The Fruit
of
Death

The Fruit of Death:

Fragments on the Theory of Sexuality

by Jean-Luc Beauchard

SENEX PRESS

Senex Press
Boston, Massachusetts
www.senexpress.org
"We publish the best books."

For the Young Fenwickians

And I pray you, my masters, be merry . . .

"The whole question of the significance of the sexual, as well as its significance in the particular spheres, has undeniably been answered poorly until now; moreover, it has seldom been answered in the correct mood. To offer witticisms about the sexual is a paltry art, to admonish is not difficult, to preach about it in such a way that the difficulty is omitted is not hard, but to speak humanly about it is an art."

~Søren Kierkegaard,
The Concept of Anxiety

Contents

Foreword
Who is the Prince?

> On the ninth or tenth night, he realized
> (with some bitterness) that nothing could be
> expected from those students who passively
> accepted his teachings, but only from those
> who might occasionally, in a reasonable way,
> venture an objection.
>
> ~Borges, "The Circular Ruins"

Jean-Luc Beauchard is an unusual character. This much is clear not only from his
various writings, but from what he takes to
be the provocations that lead him to produce
said writings. I speak not as a disinterested
party. I speak as one who has been very much
affected (I considered writing *wronged*) by
Beauchard's intellectual vendettas. My story
is not unlike the one you are about to read,
except that in the pages that follow, the author
acknowledges the inspiration for his writing—
he was miffed by something another philosopher said—whereas with me, it has mostly been
suggestion, veiled reference, and innuendo.

Only once has my adversary challenged me in the open square, and even then, he hid behind another scholar's criticism. That piece, hastily pasted onto the end of a volume I regretfully coedited—I was, admittedly, too busy at the time to review the submissions accepted by my fellow editors—is neither worth reading nor citing here. Interested parties will no doubt track it down and see for themselves just how mendacious Beauchard's critiques can be. The point of this foreword, however, is to unmask the innerworkings of a mind bent on antagonism and philosophical deceit.

It was shortly after defending my dissertation that I published my first work of philosophy. The defense itself was a harrowing affair, and once I made it out the other side, I assumed my harshest critics were behind me. Alas, it was not so. I'm not speaking of the now infamous review in the *International Journal of Philosophical Studies* (vol. 29, issue 2, pp. 259-263, for those few philistines ignorant of the slanders I've suffered). No. I'm speaking of a submission sent to the *Journal for Continental Philosophy of Religion* for which I was, at the time, acting as

Assistant Editor. (I have since been promoted to Coeditor in Chief, which, I think, bespeaks the gravity of my work, the respect of my colleagues, and my standing in the field).

The aforementioned review, penned by none other than Beauchard himself, was a scathing critique of my book *Eros Crucified*. In it, the reviewer accused me of—and I quote—"making a mockery of the cross, refusing to look the scandal of Christ's death in the face, denying the meaninglessness of our godless existence, and proposing an understanding of art, eros, and the creative impulse that can only be gleaned from the vantage point of the resurrection, a vantage point to which we have no access and of which we have no right to speak." I found the review uneven, to say the least.

Unfortunately for Beauchard, the piece received a desk rejection. It is the *Journal*'s policy, you see, not to publish reviews of its editors' work and I had no choice but to decline it. I told its author as much—in, I might add, an exceedingly collegially worded email—and he responded moments later with the following

curt message: "No matter. I see your little pam-
phlet and raise you a book of my own." I did not
know what to make of this and so, bemused and
slightly irritated, went on with my day, neglect-
ing to reply. It was only when, a little over a year
later, I opened my mail and found in it a copy of
The Mask of Memnon that I began to recognize
the peculiarity of Beauchard's person. *Memnon*, you no doubt understand, is a direct ref-
utation of my work, in particular the last three
chapters of *Eros Crucified*. Where I propose the
possibility of an "eternal present of love made
manifest *here and now*," Beauchard sees a world
in which one "finds himself [sic] caught in the
grips of sin . . . trapped, confined, unable to act,
free only to despair." Where I put forth artis-
tic creation as that which draws us "near to the
'primordial artist of the world,'" he insists upon
salvation as being proffered by "the death of
him [sic] who made us."

    To be clear, I do not wholly disagree with
Beauchard on these points. But even where
we agree, he refuses to acknowledge it. There
are no citations of *Eros Crucified* in *The Mask
of Memnon*. Indeed, my work is passed over in

utter silence. To make matters worse, he opens
the book with a note of gratitude to "all of the
thinkers who have made me what I am—and
most especially those I lovingly correct in the
pages that follow," yet does not so much as hint
at the fact that he wrote the book in response
to me! (If you doubt that my work was the cat-
alyst for his, just examine his dedication). At
least his *City of Man* references my Plato scholarship when he wants to attack it and doesn't
leave the reader in the dark about the important secondary literature I've produced. Not
that his reading of my work is charitable or
fair or even particularly rigorous or scholarly.
But I suppose some recognition is better than
the martyrdom of insignificance to which he
condemned my first monograph (published, I
might add, with a respected academic press,
ranked fourth among philosophy publishers in
the English language by the inimitable Brian
Leiter, perhaps the most precise academic of
this age).

   In any event, the point of this foreword is
not to bemoan Beauchard's glaring negligence
nor to decry his disregard for vital academic

conventions. It is rather to draw out the theological underpinnings of his work, underpinnings which may otherwise go overlooked by readers ignorant of the provocations he seems to be responding to. *City of Man*, for instance, presents itself as a thoroughly agnostic text. It says nothing about the problem of God nor seeks to inquire about the divine's relation to the human community. And yet, who could miss the resonances with Augustine? Who read Beauchard's commentary on the "philosopher king" as a kind of tyrannical shepherd of the amorphous "human herd" and not contrast it with the image of the Good Shepherd who lays down his life for his flock? Who follow the biblical references in the 23rd footnote of Book Two and not suspect that *City of Man* contains one of the most profound theological insights of the last hundred years? Who see Beauchard's repurposing of Machiavelli and not realize that the prince of whom he speaks is the prince of darkness, ruler of this world?

The Mask of Memnon, too, plays the game of veiled utterance, presenting itself as a work of literary theory when it is, upon closer inspection, an apparent attempt to revive the Christian existentialism of Kierkegaard. Beauchard seems to be putting his tongue out at readers, saying of Barthes' *La mort de l'auteur,* "And let us not forget that concealed beneath this work of literary theory is a work of theology"—a phrase which ought rightly to be directed at *Memnon* itself. In true metareal fashion, he tells readers what he's up to by attributing his best insights to another, bequeathing his own thinking to a distorted image of someone else in order to mask what he really means to say. Is this "indirect communication," *à la* the contemporary poet Louis Light? Without question it is. And like a child of Light, Beauchard mixes means with ends, inviting readers to pursue their desire to discover what's been hidden— like one stumbling upon a treasure buried in a field—and promising that those who are patient enough to seek shall be rewarded with extraordinary finds.

As for the present text, its theological import is readily available, if only one persists in withholding judgment until the end. The stark view of human sexuality presented in its

opening fragments is complemented and complicated by its closing reflections on the virginity of Mary. But, as with sex itself, one must be
willing to wait and prolong one's anticipation
in order to enjoy this work's ripest fruits. And
yet, who can withhold judgment when talking
about sex? Who withstand the salacious invita-
tion to read into the text one's own desires and
so see in it not what it says but what one wants
it to say, just as each of us is guilty of reading
into the words of another the echoes of our own
longing, especially when we long for that other
to mirror back to us our own desires?

Am I speaking in riddles? Perhaps. But
if so, that is because this work, like all of
Beauchard's writings, has bewitched me. Lur-
ing me in with the promise of finding myself,
assuring me that if only I read carefully, I will
be able to better understand my own thinking,
it has left me with the image of another—one
whom I do not recognize and yet somehow
know, as if I've met him before, if only in a
dream, as if I were walking alongside him on
the road and he was hooded, concealing his
face, telling me secrets I've thought but never

dared to understand. A mad image? To be sure. Mad in the way that all wisdom is mad. Mad with the folly inspired by desire—but, if we follow our author closely on this point, that folly is inspired by divine desire, an eros crucified and (who knows?) perhaps even resurrected, regardless of whether or not our Fr. Beauchard is willing to admit it.

M. Saverio Clemente
March 30, 2023
Feast of St. John of the Ladder

With Gratitude

One rarely considers how much life goes into the making of a book. Of course, authors never tire of telling us that they poured themselves into every page. And of course, it's not uncommon for them to thank their editors, their agents, the presses that publish their works. But what about the cover artist? What about the bookbinder? Or, today, the manufacturer of the bookbinding machine? What about those who mined the material to make that machine and those who transported it from the mine to the factory in which it was processed to another factory and another until the machine was made? What about the ink makers? What about the workers in the papermill? And the paper—where did it come from? The truck drivers who hauled the lumber? The loggers? The tree farmers? The trees themselves? No one considers the trees, how they went like a lamb to the slaughter, how they laid down their lives for the sake of a book.

In Christian spirituality, it is not uncommon to hear mention of "the wood of the cross." In certain sects, supplicants are even encouraged to spend time on Good Friday kneeling before a wooden replica of the crucifix and showering it with kisses. But one never hears talk of the tree that died to make the wood God died upon. Is that not a glaring omission? Are not our books made of the Tree of Knowledge of Good and Evil? How willingly it dies so we can read and prosper thereby. How lovingly it lays down its life, as if it were doing so for a friend. Will the tree rise like the Risen Lord? Can it too receive its life back again? It can and it will a hundredfold, if the book it died for is worthy of its sacrifice.

This is the goal of every true author—that his work should evince the gratitude demanded by the sacrifices of those who gave their lives to make it. May this humble little book live up to that awesome demand. And if not, may its author be forgiven.

Preface

Dear Reader,

Imagine, if you will, a beetle. Or, rather, imagine the unfortunate Mr. Gregor Samsa after he metamorphosed into a giant bug. Now imagine that somewhere by his protruding gaster, there is a small appendage (I call it "small" not by comparison to the same appendages on other insects, but only in proportion to the antennae, legs, and the rest of Mr. Samsa's body), so small, in fact, that you hardly notice it, even as you suffer to gaze upon his insectile frame. Now imagine that Mr. Samsa is so enthralled, so obsessed with one particular function of that little *funiculus* that he bases the most significant decisions of his life upon it and spends the better part of his days thinking about it—something that, incidentally, no insect would ever do (although I admittedly know precious little about insects, except for what I've read in Aesop, which I haven't read in years, but which—if memory serves (admittedly, a big *if*, especially at my age)–I hold to be demonstrably true).

Would you not find such behavior surprising? Would you not say it was strange and (I say this disinterestedly, without the slightest hint of judgment or moralization) kind of pathetic and sad? Would you not perhaps laugh to see how much significance Mr. Samsa invests in so small an appendage? Perhaps an insect would behave this way–like a man–if it had a human mind. For it is not so much the *funiculus* as such that consumes our energies, both physical and psychical, but rather the "fun" of the *funiculus*, so to speak, that is, the symbolic value we ascribe to it, a symbolic value around which we have built whole civilizations, so much so that one cannot take sex out of the city–it lies at the very foundation of things, comingled with the blood of Abel, killed by the hand of his brother, the same hand that built the first city and then proceeded to do God knows what else. (On this, and other related topics, see my recent book *City of Man*, an exceedingly charming read, I assure you). Sex, I argue here, borrows its violence from that foundational act of civilization

and not against it. Sex, like murder, is a form of
destruction wrought from the mind of man and
carried out with dirty hands.

~

The present text is an homage to Søren
Kierkegaard and to his character-author
Johannes Climacus who, as St. John of the
Sinai Monastery, left us a book called *Climax*,
that is, the *Ladder*. The following forty fragments should also be read as a kind of ladder,
a climax that takes a bit longer, not because it
ascends higher than the climax of Climacus,
but because it begins lower, much lower, in the
subterranean regions of the soul.

The challenge here—and, if you'll allow
me to sing my own praises, the *artistry*—was to
write in as condensed a form as possible, say,
on a single page, what might have been easier
said in an entire chapter. So came to be these
"fragments" which contain the *rationes semina-
les* of the whole. But since the *whole* has been for
a long time now confused with the *systematic*,
let it instead be fragmented like the Plotinian
One into these *Fragments*. Historically, it has

been the job of the poets to break things down
and exalt their singularity and multiplicity.
("These fragments I have shored against my
ruins" and so on). That might help to explain
why these *Fragments* sound, at times, a little
too poetical. They are not, however, poems, and
they make no pretensions to poetry. Rather,
they are a series of quasi-phenomenological
observations (surprising, strange, and sad) on
human sexuality, developed in a strict dialecti-
cal fashion.

I should note that this book originates, as
all great books do, from a dispute. After reading—and being profoundly disturbed by—an
essay from my esteemed colleague at the College of the Holy Cross, J. Manoussakis, I decided
that someone needed to counter his distorted
description of sexual desire—and who better
to do so than *me*? That essay, published in the
two-thousand-nineteenth year of our Lord,
under the somewhat verbose title "Dying to
Desire. *Soma*, *Sema*, *Sarx*, and *Sex*" in a volume
called *Somatic Desire: Recovering Corporeality in
Contemporary Thought*, edited by Sarah Horton
et al. by Lexington Books (pp. 117–137), ought

xxiv   Jean-Luc Beauchard

not to have been written, let alone be read. (I have confidence that you, dear reader, will resist the temptation to go to your nearest device and look it up). In the interest and service of fairness, I sent these humble *Fragments* to Professor Manoussakis as soon as I had completed them—I wanted him to know how mistaken he was—and, to his credit, he replied to my correction of his errors with a full retraction, included as a *Postscript* below.

JLB
Fenwick University
July 31, 2023
Feast of St. Ignatius of Loyola

Fragment I

If someone were to strike up a conversation with me about sex—say, after reading something I had written on the subject—I would consider his doing so to be in bad taste. It would make me uncomfortable, for instance, if my interlocutor spoke to me of his (or anyone else's) sex life. Ask me, however, about sex *in general* and watch me talk—or, in this case, write—boldly and eloquently, with confidence and authority.

Let us note this inconsistency, this peculiarity, as one characteristic, among many others, of sex. And it is noteworthy because it goes against the norms that govern our other social interactions. As a rule, we are keener to talk to others about our recent trip to Paris, that is, to talk about *our* Paris, *our* experience of Paris, than unleash on them a number of general insights *about* Paris, while maintaining all along an ambiguous silence about whether we have ever visited the City of Delights ourselves.

Fragment 2

Safety Precaution: The scientist who handles a deadly virus would do well to protect himself. He ought to wear gloves, a mask, and other such personal protective equipment; but I need nothing less than a distance of at least two millennia of history to handle sex *safely*—that is, in order to talk about it, as if it were a thing of the past, a cultural phenomenon of an ancient civilization long forgotten, something Plato wrote about in his *Phaedrus* and *Symposium* and not something happening all around me, in rooms on the other side of my neighbors' windows, in the bedrooms of my dearest friends, in private and public spaces, in cars on my street corner, and even (who knows?) in the building in which I live.

Fragment 3

A unique topic. How to approach it? Here at once an epistemological problem of the first order—that is, a problem that has to do with the very metaphysical foundation of the epistemic—presents itself: I am referring to the problematic status of the knower or the observer. To oversimplify, it is always a mind that thinks about how minds think, and failing to take this paradox into account leads to the kind of risible epistemological blindness the best examples of which can be found in *scientific*—read, *objective*—accounts of religion and religious phenomena. The folly of the scientist (the *social* scientist!) can be gleaned in this: he profanes the mysteries he studies by attempting to examine them from *without*, as if he weren't involved.

It is vital that we remain mindful of this as we attempt to approach the topic of sex, as our inquiry can only be pursued along similar paths, through a form and medium distant from the topic at hand—that is, the non-sexual.

It makes more sense, you might say—you erotic reader, you—to approach sex *sexually*. (How can one understand the City of God if one hasn't dwelt in it?). Alas, this, I'm afraid, cannot be easily done, especially not in a book which stands, after all, in the place and in lieu of such an impossible encounter with the reader.

But never mind that. Noting the caveat of a limitation imposed by the nature of our approach, we must insist that our observations still stand. And so, they do.

Fragment 4

It might be worth observing that everything about sex is *disproportional*: disproportionally important in our obsession with it—no longer a merely private affair, since talk of it permeates public discourse—at the same time and *contra* its ubiquity, disproportionally demonized and censored; the place it occupies, disanalogously great; unfairly suppressed, whenever it is so, but also incorrectly praised and exalted; widely discussed, yet no better understood; either dismissed too fast, or indulged for too long.

Why this? Why, when it comes to sex, do we fail to get the proportions right? What is it about sex that disturbs, so to speak, the gravitational force that things usually exercise upon us? Why does sex affect such a great distortion? Whether we have an answer to this question or not, and regardless of what that answer might be, we will be well-advised to take notice of this *distortion* as *an essential characteristic of sex.*

5

[Nota bene: *In another sense, one can say the same about love. Isn't distortion an essential characteristic of love as well? Think of the blindness of eros—or the blindness inflicted by eros—the Eros who possesses us like those other deities of the Greeks who personify such destructive (always self-destructive) drives as Lyssa and Mania. Eros the irrational who drives men mad.*]

Fragment 5

The sexual *intentionality*, that is, the sexual orientation of consciousness, especially in its interactions with other subjects, is, as a potential, always *there*. That is, no matter who the other person is in himself or in his relation to me, I perceive him through the lens of a sexual intentionality. True, such a sexual intentionality toward the other is only one of many other various (*all-various*, you might say) characteristics and, on occasion, it might be the one of least importance; but it is there and, what is more, it has been systematically avoided in our phenomenological analyses of everyday intersubjectivity. This does not mean that in my everyday interactions with other people I perceive each as potential objects of my sexual desire, but it does mean that I perceive every person as a sexual being *like me*.

In my unacknowledged—and, if it makes you, dear reader, more comfortable, I would be happy to say *disinterested*—curiosity about what role the other may or may not play in the sexual sphere, in guessing, on the basis of so many subtle, indeed very subtle signs that the other unavoidably presents about his sexual tastes, preferences, and practices, engaging, as it were, in an endless hermeneutics of "sexualization"—endless because the variations through which human sexuality manifests and materializes itself are themselves infinite—I already perceive the other in his horizon of sexuality from which neither I nor he can be extricated as long as we both remain bodily beings. If what I just called "the horizon of sexuality" presents me with the other as a sexual object (by which, I mean a "sexualized" being) through his body, it is, nevertheless, not on account of his body (or mine, for that matter) that the other appears always inscribed in a sexual horizon or through a sexual intentionality. The reason for that lies instead with that essential character of consciousness that seeks to affirm its subjectivity by objectifying another or by objectifying itself for another.

Fragment 6

One of the necessary clarifications—a distinction that must be made prior to any meaningful discussion of sex—is the fact that when we talk about sex, we don't talk about the mechanics of sex as such, but about the "with whom" and the "how" and "where" and "when" of sex, which are not merely conditions, but the real object/objective of sexual desire. For, if we were to propose a substitution of sex with sex, but insist upon the omission of what one takes to be accidental, namely, the "how," the "where," the "when," and the "with whom," then what would be left—some other version of sex—would invariably fail to attract our interest. Which means that *sex* does not denote a universal desire or even an act that could be defined or described without the non-sexual conditions of one's desire. *It is what appears to be entirely peripheral to sex that determines my sexual desire.*

Fragment 7

The pleasure of sex is not sexual pleasure.
It wouldn't be an exaggeration to say that for most people, or at least for some—let each of us be a philosopher and decide for himself—their lives are structured, one way or another, around the advent of sexual pleasure. Why is sex pleasurable? It feels good. But it is not the only experience that does. Perhaps, then, it is not only the pleasure of sex that counts, but also its intensity. Sex is an intense pleasure. But even with intensity taken into account, sex is not, as far as intense pleasures go, so superior to the pleasure associated with the daily evacuation of one's bowels. And yet, the toilet industry has never come close to the notoriety and popularity of the pornography industry.

There must, therefore, be something more, something else, that accounts for the extraordinary power of sex. It is not that sex keeps us more captive to the pleasures of the flesh than other (bodily or not) pleasures. In fact, sex is not carnal at all. For, it is precisely in the intensity of sexual pleasure that the body takes leave from its senses. It takes leave from its senses because it is overpowered by them. For a moment there is no body anymore, only pleasure—that is, only sensing, an anonymous sense. Like every instrument, the body achieves and serves its purpose best when it completely disappears in the act—*ready-to-hand, zuhandenheit.*

Fragment 8

The pleasure of sex is not sexual pleasure. Rather, the distinct quality that accounts for the pleasure of sex lies furthest from the body, in role-playing. Role-playing, which is so characteristic of sex, from the most innocent to the most perverse of its manifestations (and it is precisely this common element that renders the differentiation between these two useless), derives its importance, so much so as to be an essential characteristic of it, from the archetypical role-playing, that of the Subject/Object dialectic. Sex is pleasurable because there is a Subject I am and an Object I want to be treated as, and because there is a Subject you are and an Object I want to treat you as. By allowing us to engage in this role-playing, which, as with all role-*playing*, is also a role-*exchanging*, sex exposes the Subject and the Object (or better still, the subjectivity of the subject and the objectivity of the object) as mere roles, which, like Genet's *Les Bonnes*, have no claim to a further, more substantial reality.

The pleasure of sex, then, consists in its being a kind of play (as much dramatic and theatrical as playful) in which and through which we overthrow both the roles and the rules of subjectivity. It is in this sense only that it is correct to say that sex, in all its variations, is ecstatic. But the transcendence of sexual ecstasy is not a movement toward an encounter with the other (for there is no other in sex) but the effort, always only briefly successful, to escape from the self.

Fragment 9

The pleasure of sex is not sexual pleasure. The pleasure of sex does not lie in the sexual act, but in what comes next. In other words, if we were to locate sexual pleasure, we would locate it *after* sex. Of course, there is the pleasure of anticipating the sexual act, which, at times, is also more pleasurable than sex, and there is the pleasure that comes with the actualization of a fantasy that was, up until that moment, only possible and only given in the imagination—although, as with everything, and especially with everything that our imagination has magnified beyond its real proportions and our expectation has intensified by raising it to unrealistic heights, realization tends to leave us disappointed. In both cases, however, that of anticipatory and that of realized pleasure, the pleasure derives from the pleasure that lies after the sexual act and which we Frenchmen aptly call *la petit mort*. For it is, as we have argued above, the

14

death of the self, of ourselves, that we seek to
bring about by sex.

Fragment 10

The pleasure of sex is not sexual pleasure.
The pleasure of sex is that παῦσις (a
κατάπαυσις, a *sabbatism* of sorts) that
Aristophanes mentions, as a μηχανή in the *Symposium*. There is more here than homeostasis.
There is *rest*, the cessation or suspension of
subjectivity. To compare it, for the sake of illustration, to the rise and fall of Sisyphus's boulder, the pleasure of sex is not reaching the apex
of the hill—that is, the orgasm or climax *per
se*—but the state that comes after, namely, the
moment between the rock's descent and Sisyphus's first step, repeated already infinitely,
the moment before he returns to his task which
awaits him at the bottom of the hill. For that
moment, however brief, after the release and
before the new dawn of tension, Sisyphus is
no-one. And *contra* Camus, for people like Sisyphus, such a moment of non-existence is the
only glimpse of happiness.

[Nota bene: *According to Homer, Sisyphus is κέρδιστος ἀνδρῶν, that is, the "most gaining among men," a reference to the capital gains he was able to make as the founder of Corinth and the first to control the Isthmus of Corinth, thus becoming (as Ruskin observes in* Queen of Air*) "the type of transit, transfer, or trade." It is in the underworld that Sisyphus finds out the true meaning of the proverbial phrase about the "rolling stone" which not only, as we all know, "gathers no moss" but also finds no rest in all eternity.*]

Fragment 11

When we said that the ecstatic character of sex is an escape from the self rather than an encounter with the other—as those who, like Clemente, would like to domesticate or justify sex by modeling it after the interpersonal relationship would have us believe—we did not contradict ourselves, as it might seem, by also maintaining that an essential characteristic of sex is the (by definition dyadic) dialectic of the Subject/Object role-play. Indeed, sex always necessitates (at least) two, even in its solitary approximation. But the other in sex is merely another position in the bipolar structure of the role-playing. For, in order for sexual role-play to be a play between roles, one must be able to occupy the other's position, which is, as should be clear, only *the other* position. The Object is a variable of the Subject and not the Subject's other, or a being that is otherwise than the Subject. The Object is defined by subjectivity in the sense that there is an Object only for a Subject.

Similarly, in sex—as Plato's *Phaedrus* describes in great detail—the beloved, the sexual partner, whether numerically one or more, real or imaginary, is therefore only the occasion that holds, symbolically, as it were, the place of the "there" by which I can orientate my "here" and from which I can change positions between "here" and "there," between the Subject and the Object that keep changing places.

Fragment 12

Proof of this—*that sex is not carnal and that role-playing is an essential characteristic of sex*—is provided by pornography's classification of sex into categories, all of which are non-sexual. This ought to make clear that sex always operates within a non-sexual context, a context that functions as an imaginary background for every sexual encounter. Just as, in a minimalist staging of a theatrical play the branch of a tree might represent a whole forest, so do these non-sexual categories set the scene for sex.

Fragment 13

Proof of this—*that what sex seeks to accomplish is an escape from oneself*—is the fact that, if this flight from the self can be accomplished in a different way—say through the secular or sacred addictions of the junkie and the saint—then sex itself loses its appeal.

Fragment 14

The desire to become another Subject's Object and the pleasure that comes from being objectified, and so abused, should not strike us as paradoxical: there still lies an *intensification*, so to speak, of the Subject's sovereignty, in abdicating one's claim to subjectivity, for one *makes oneself* an object. This self-making of the self contains inside it all the Luciferian pride of a Prometheus: *Behold! I am the Subject that has the power to turn himself into an Object!*

Fragment 15

The image that one finds in *Genesis* and in the *Phaedrus* of one's sperm spilt on the ground, buried in the ground, where it dies and cannot bring forth fruit, was a clear hint at the *suicidal* character of masturbation. Self-satisfaction toward sex and toward death. But masturbation is, fundamentally, pleasant. Thus, a beyond is inscribed in the pleasure principle.

Fragment 16

It makes sense that incest (and all its variations) is by far the most prolific phantasy. It makes sense, if you think that the sexual organ is, at the same time, the same as the reproductive organ. And so, inevitably, the sexual act invokes one's own origin and generation and, thereby, its shadow—namely, one's death.

Fragment 17

In condemning the pervert, we make the mistake of taking him as *one of a kind* rather than what he really is, *one of a species*. But since we, as it happens, belong to the same species, it is better to condemn *our* vice, made manifest in this other individual, than pretend we are exempt from it.

Fragment 18

O ne characteristic of sexuality has escaped our notice entirely. It is only concerning sex that, among all other pleasures of the flesh, one prefers its *simulation*—by that I mean its onanistic and pornographic substitution—to the act itself. Consider: If one were to take pleasure in watching other people eat from a sumptuous and variegated menu, featuring dishes ranging from the most common and familiar to the rarest and most exotic, while satisfying his hunger by masticating on air until he reaches satiety; if, from that point on, he had no appetite for any kind of food, whether real or imaginary, even though he remained as empty-stomached as before; if he did this every day and would rather do it than enjoy an actual meal, would we treat it as casually as we now treat the fact that in sex one is entirely content with the imaginary?

What does this mean? Doesn't it suggest that the pleasure of sex even in reality derives from the imaginary? In which case, it is rather the sexual act itself that is the substitution of the original pleasure of pornography. What does it mean, then, to say that pornography is more original than sex? It means that sexual pleasure is the pleasure of a transgression, namely, the pleasure of seeing that which one is not allowed to see and knowing that which is the object of forbidden knowledge. (The subtle reader will recognize this point from another work of mine—and you, I know, are a subtle reader). Perhaps for this reason eating from the forbidden tree has always been seen as an allegory, if not merely an allusion, that conceals the primordial guilt of sex. This suggestion is nearly correct, except it gets the order all wrong: sex is the allegory, the ritual dance that re-enacts dramatically (and I feel tempted to write "even liturgically") the eating of the forbidden fruit.

Fragment 19

There have always been two things human beings are not supposed to be able to do and they both have to do with one's bed. (Perhaps that's why it is eerie to watch yourself sleep). There have always been two inviolable conditions for human existence. One can see, and perhaps must see, another die, but no man can see *himself* die; and one can see another having sex, but no man has been able to see *himself* having sex. Until now.

No private man, I should say, for with the advent of photographic reproduction, it became possible for some—the professionals—to record themselves having sex and to display it to themselves and others. They were still considered *actors*, however. Actors who, strictly speaking, were presenting characters, not themselves. It is only in the wake of this generation that, for the first time in human history, one (indeed, *every*one) can record, share and post publicly what was meant to be kept private even from one's own eyes. One begins to recognize the historical importance of this first time, the first of almost a new *kind* of a human being who, having succeeded in watching himself, as if he was another, having sex, might also, in due time, *watch himself die*.

In any case, reality itself has now become a porn category—and that completes the system.

Fragment 20

Is the difference between sex and pornography only the fact that the latter is a representation of the former? Is, in other words, the relation between the sexual act and its representation as simple as, say, that of the original to its copy or of the thing itself to its semblance? If so, it would seem that the enjoyment of the representation could not constitute an act—*if* it could be said to be an act at all—comparable to the act represented, as the reader of a murder mystery who enjoys reading about a good crime is not, normally, guilty of the crime he reads about. Let it be said then that to think about something does not amount to doing it and that reflection remains always separated from action and actuality.

And yet—we *feel* that the enjoyment of pornography engages a pleasure that we recognize as similar to, if not the same as, that of the enjoyment of sex. The distinction I have just described, the distinction between, to use phenomenological language, the reflecting and the reflected becomes blurry here. What is more, the original distinction—the distinction between pornography and sex, for it was upon this distinction that their difference was established—namely, the distinction between public and private, is likewise obscure.

"Porn" comes from the Greek word for brothel (*porneion*), which in turn comes from the verb πέρνημι that signifies the selling and buying of sex, that is, sex "gone public" as we say today of a company that has joined the marketplace. And that's exactly it: a *porneion* was the sex market of the ancient world, just as pornography, in all its Protean manifestations, both physical and digital, is a sex market for the modern. A sex market so much more efficient and effective than its ancient counterpart for it is free and *ubiquitous*. It is due to the emergence of the digital world that the distinction between private and public has been reversed in recent years. A crucial reversal whereby one *first* introduces oneself to strangers with one's genitals, and only after some measure of confidence has been established, with his face.

Interlude

Some Aphorisms
on Writing and Life

It is a mistake to think the book
gives us the author.
At most, it gives us the author's character,
a mask made by the man who wears it.

Chastity is the opposite of prudishness.
But a prudish world knows not why.

Seeing one's life not as one life—one
possibility among many—but as life itself and
judging others thereby is the sin
of which we all are guilty.

On delivering a manuscript to the press:
There are things to love in it, things to hate,
and I've lost the will to make changes.

The greatest ideas, like the greatest jokes,
make for the best secrets.

To be more radical than the radicals,
one need only be more honest.

One must resist the temptation to align one-
self with a school of thought.
One cannot be Beauchardian.
One can only be Beauchard.

Illusions are only illusions until they are real.

To become the butt of one's own joke is to
realize one's greatest potential.

To know oneself as sinner is to know oneself
as saint.

The only thing more tragic than dying too
soon is dying too late.

We're all in favor of dialogue—until
we disagree.

Style attracts attention. Thought fixes it.

For the artist, nothing is wasted.

We all love morality—especially our own.
Disinterest is the scholar's deceit.

Ambivalence is love.

Confusing the confused is as pleasant as it is
simple.

The artist is never bored.

Sanctity is dangerous.
One must conceal it more than one's sins.

To live in an age that lacks
the Great Philosopher
is a sin against philosophers.
Where does today's Pascal go
to find his Descartes?
Where today's Kierkegaard to find his Hegel?

The philosopher who risks himself is liable to
be wrong more often than right. So be it.

Every misfire is summed up and atoned for
with the rare hit of the mark.

Great writers demand greater readers as
recompense for their labor.
Never underestimate the lengths to which man
will go to ruin things.

Man is never quite so beautiful as when he
shows his pallid face.

That years of work can be dismissed offhand
by cursory readings is more painful than
surprising to the author of merit.

The truly great author cannot be categorized.
He is a world unto himself.

That indulging desire does nothing to assuage
it but rather inflames it is one of those plain
facts no one wants to know.

Sin is the expression of a pain that cannot or
will not be named.

It is no mercy to mask poison with sugar.

Reading is a spiritual exercise.

One can only blaspheme against false gods.

Irreverence is an expression of faith.

One generation's condemnation of the last
evinces a failure of imagination rather than
strong moral character.

Not to inflict suffering when one is content is
hard. Not to inflict suffering when one is
suffering is impossible.

Academic rigor has much to recommend it,
as do all the worst vices.

It is amusing to see people adopt insults as
titles. Academic, for instance. And professor.

Not knowing is the scholar's area of expertise.

That kindness can be felt as cruelty and cruelty kindness is one of the great perils of human existence.

Beware the man with an ax to grind. He's liable to test his blade on your throat.

Media is for today. Art is for tomorrow.

Universities dedicate resources to creative writing yet undervalue that finer art, creative reading.

Opium is now the opiate of the masses. Three cheers for progress!

That a thing is likely to happen does not mean it will. That it is unlikely does not mean it won't. A lesson for statisticians.

Not letting life stand in the way of one's aspirations or not letting one's aspirations stand in the way of life—which is harder?

Both the idolization of and disdain for the great thinkers of the past reveals the same lowness of spirit. It is true that the author of today will never do what they did. It is equally true that they could never have done what today's author does.

The need to make things right can be as destructive as the wrong done.

Being right is a vice.

Man is the dying animal.
His triumph is to know it.

Cynicism is a mask for pain.

Satire is comedy with a sneer.

Nihilism is a luxury the wretched cannot afford.

Precision in language precedes style.

Saints live for the impossible.

More malice originates from dyspepsia than hatred.

It is a mistake to conflate the author with his characters. Characters exist to perfect the author—both his virtues and his vices.

Attendere aude.

Humility is its own form of hubris.

There is no law dictating that the narcissist can't also be right.

Speaking truth to power maintains the economy of power. Christ was silent before Pilate.

Few things enliven thought more than the attempt to grasp political man. Nothing deadens thought more than to become him.

Suffering is heuristic. And if you can't learn from yours, others will.

We all love the ignoble lie that we could have without creating, *eo ipso*, have-nots.

It is not the thought, but the gift that counts.

The poet is the true alchemist, his mixtures more golden than gold.

Not bread and circuses but license and justification are what the people want.

You're surprised to learn he justifies himself with his philosophy? My friend, why else would he cultivate the art?

Humility is a rope suspended between resentment and pride.

The first job of every author is to delight.

How charming it is to discover that everything you've been told about a given thinker is wrong.

It is not senseless suffering but sensible
suffering that ought to confound.

Philosophers rarely rely on their best
argument because that would mean having
to live it.

The only thing sadder than becoming a
caricature is to be one without knowing it.

The belief in one's ability to fix things is the
greatest temptation and the greatest folly.

Every sentence that begins with "I was"
has the potential to devastate.

Forgiveness is a kind of death and it is the
resurrection of the dead.

For the lie to be believable, it must be true.

Fear of death signifies a love of life.
And yet how unlovable it makes it.

Grace: Refusing to vent one's fears and one's
sadness on others.

The law is like a good walking stick:
Stabilizing on a treacherous path, but
necessary to leave behind as one makes
the ascent.

He who writes satires must take care not to
become one.

The solitary genius attracts admirers,
the true genius—friends.

Distrust the man who offers you answers.

You catch more flies with honey than arsenic,
but the point is to kill flies, isn't it?

One must read scholarship to know for certain
what the text does not say.

You're far too serious to be taken seriously.

Complacency is a temptation, comfort a tomb.

Courage is a noble lie.

It is strange to discover how pious everyone is, especially the impious.

The greatest wars are fought for the stupidest reasons.

Writing Instructor: Write what you know.

Socrates: I know nothing.

The genius knows how much effort it takes to make genius look effortless.

There are as many men who once had potential as women who once had beauty—and most lost theirs for the same reason.

To divorce the literary from the philosophical is to undermine both.

Our novelists have failed us as spectacularly as our philosophers. Neither teach that good writing and good thinking are one.

To be yourself is the greatest disguise.

To assert oneself is human. To deny oneself
divine.

The artist's vocation is to make his first piece
his masterpiece. Every subsequent piece
as well.

The need to be taken seriously is a thoroughly
unserious pursuit.

Sins can be explained and even forgiven but
never excused.

Rules are only rules when you get caught.

The best works are written with one's life.

Fortune smiles on those who believe.

Pride says *I* when honesty says *we*.

There are authors who will write entire books
simply for the cover.

Most of man's problems can be attributed to
his being too young.

If they love you, they will hate you.

The best authors don't write—*they sing*.

An intelligent man can speak on many topics
but rarely speaks on any.

To be quoted is to be misquoted.

Those who promise to change
ought to change their promises.

Beyond the philosopher's *Why?* is the artist's
Why not?

Fragment 21

Thoughts come *to* us, not *from* us. Thinking is fundamentally receptive. It is not, as we tend to imagine, productive. But if that is true, we ought to be careful about which thoughts we allow to enter through the gates of our minds. And even though all thinking, as Heidegger suggests, consists of the hospitality of thanksgiving, still, to welcome in evil—and make no mistake, to entertain an evil thought is to welcome it, as Ruskin writes, "into your own heart" (see, also, my reading of the myth of the ring of Gyges)—is to welcome something that has "power against you which your health and virtue depend on your resisting" (again, Ruskin). This, perhaps, explains Plato's misgivings about art. On this point, the *Republic* stands vindicated—and not only on this point, right, my friend?

It is also a point that needs to be taken into our consideration of sex and, in particular, the role of the pornographic attitude, an attitude which is in fact very much present in every manifestation of the sexual and not merely in watching porn. Such an attitude—which not only violates the rule of privacy and, like Pentheus, desires to see what is not permissible to see, thus making sex sacrilegious, a *concupiscentia oculorum* that retains, even when it turns its searching gaze to "secular" matters, its blasphemous character—*invites* evil into one's mind by thinking it. But to think— is this really a less effective means of bringing something to life, of making the fictive real?

Evil? one might retort. *Can we really speak of evil—we who have liberated ourselves from right and wrong?* Yes, very good. That is indeed a point I have assumed. You have found me out. I was speaking from the pulpit and taking for granted a notion of sin. And yet, any true reader of mine knows that I have a complicated understanding of sin. But never mind that. Let us refer instead to the example, mentioned just above, of the unhappy—for that is what his name means—Pentheus, King of Thebes. Pentheus, who profanes the sacred secrecy of Dionysus' maenads by gazing upon them, but—and note this—precisely without being watched in return. Pentheus, who indulges the pornographic desire to see without being seen, playing the part of spectator who watches from a safe distance, shielded from the eyes of others. Pentheus, mounted upon his fir-tree, looking down upon the sacred orgy of everyday people, whether "professional" or "amateur," engaging in their Dionysian orgies—is the behavior of Pentheus not as sinful as the best and most proper conception of sin that one can find in all of Greek tragedy? Is his not the sin of *hubris*?

But today's profanations, one might retort, *happen long before we modern Pentheuses have the chance to view them. In most cases, the Dionysian orgiasts themselves profane their sacred rites by posting them on the internet for any peeping Pentheus to see.* Again, you are right, dear reader, as astute as you are charming in your objections. Sadly, it's true that when it comes to sex—and many other things besides—we have lost the sense of the secret: "ἐπὶ τοῖσδε πωλοῦμεν τὴν ἱερωσύνην τοῦ Διονύσου."[1]

---

1   "On these conditions, we sell Dionysus's priesthood"—thus reads the opening of a 2nd century B.C. inscription found on the wall of a subterranean shrine (καταγώγιον) at Priene.

Fragment 22

One can hardly think of a more emphatic, unambiguous form of assent than sexual arousal and, *Deo volente*, orgasm. The pornographic attitude is never innocent in the sense of the spectator's neutrality with regard to the crimes that unfold on stage. Porn always implicates the viewer. But even in theater, pleasure, as much as Aristotle's "pity and piety" (*Poetics*, 1449b25), suggests not mere empathy, but involvement.

Fragment 23

This is a "hard saying" (John 6:60) and "a hard thing to ask" (2 Kings 2:10) but, nevertheless, it is true. There is no doubt that sexual arousal ought to be, in the body's language, the strongest form of assent. (For the moment I am interested only in the epistemological *assent* and not the ethical *consent*). The notion that one does not actually participate in the sexual phantasmagoria simply because he doesn't partake in what one clearly enjoys is a sophism. His arousal betrays him. His pleasure confirms it. He might as well have done *it* himself. (And let the reader's imagination as well as his own personal experience determine the unspeakable acts to which that *it* refers).

Fragment 24

We must say something about the reduction of sex into an exclusively recreational pleasure, one among many others and nothing more. There is plenty of evidence, furnished by literature and archeology, to suggest that this was not always the case. There is consistent evidence that suggests that sex was considered sacred, whether it was connected with ancient religious rituals or with civic and political rites of initiation. In all of these functions, now entirely lost, sex was and remained sacred because it was protected as a secret.

The sense of secrecy, violated by pornography—that is, the notion of privacy (today understood only in the thinnest of terms, i.e., legally)—maintained sex's sacredness, even if, in the hands of a blasphemous man, the sacred could be made to look monstrous or grotesque. There is no such fear today, for there can be no possibility of committing a blasphemy if there is nothing sacred left to sex. Having become public, having entered the marketplace, the agora, "with an uncovered head," it has acquired a *price* and it is now everywhere *sold*.

As for pornography proper, I would categorize it as a kind of magic along with other dark arts that traffic in the occult and demonic because, first, it is predicated on a desire to look at what is not permissible to see (that is, it invites *a gaze that profanes*) and, second, it offers a promise that is *instantaneously* gratified. (On the connection between the *instant* and the *demonic*, see Kierkegaard). That latter aspect it shares with modern technology; but pornography has always been technological—insofar as it presupposes some form of technology, however primitive—as, conversely, technology has always been, to some extent, pornographic in the voyeuristic thrust that motivates all its tele-visions.

Fragment 25

I would like to claim that the only act of
political resistance today, the only genuine
and effective revolution against the Market
and its ability to reduce everything to prod-
uct, is abstinence. If you don't like the current
market-serving, capitalist configuration of
the world, if you can't condone the injustices
it breeds, you should be prepared to attack it
at its Achille's heel—the only spot it is vulnera-
ble—namely, sex.

Let me explain by going back to Aristophanes' insight in the *Symposium* about παῦσις—
this word, so crucial to our understanding of the
role sex plays in Plato—and also by noting that
Plato, as a Greek, understands sex as a political category. Let us try to think how a "hold"
(a "pause") on sex pauses the entire economic
system of generation and production—the car
industry, for example, which is predicated
on our desire for the object to transcend its
function of transportation and to make us, car
owners, more (sexually) desirable. Or think,

for example, of the "health" industry—health clubs, supplements, diets, cosmetics. Are they not supported solely by our vanity, our need to appear more attractive? Add to this the whole world of fashion, jewelry, spas, resorts, and so on. If we decide to abstain from sex, we are no longer customers seeking these products and services. We have extricated ourselves from their economy, we are worthless to them and, more importantly, they are worthless to us. For what they sell, they sell by capitalizing on our desire to be desirable.

Each of us has proven, time and again, how difficult it is to resist the temptation: "Buy this and you shall be liked." Civilizations have risen and fallen in pursuit of a beautiful Helen. Even those "goods" which we believe to be pursued for their own sake, such as power, fame, and wealth, are seen in the eyes of those who love them as bestowing that elusive (and all-important) quality of making their possessor *likable*.

It is amazing what we are willing to do, how far we are willing to go in order to be (or, more accurately, to be considered) attractive. We amass wealth to be attractive. We deprive ourselves of happiness by subjecting ourselves to all kinds of physical and mental pain to be attractive. And what does this "to be attractive" mean if not to become the object of the other's desire? Why are we so desperate to become the object of the other's desire? What does desire mean to its objects, what does it make us that we would want it so badly? To have the recognition (as in Hegelian dialectics) of having a self? Is all desire a selfish desire, i.e., the desire of a self in need of self-affirmation?

Fragment 26

Sex as μηχανή μελέτης in the *Symposium. A propos* this observation of William Reich in *The Function of the Orgasm*: "my clinical work had convinced me that the sexually gratified are also the more productive in the cultural sense." Of course, that was the very point of the second divine intervention upon the human body's anatomy in Aristophanes' telling: the gods made it so that human beings could have sex and then return to the *polis*, become inscribed within its economic structure, that is, as Reich argues, become re-*productive*. In that sense, the only honest revolt against capitalism is abstinence.

[Nota bene: *Clemente is right (for once) when he says that* "sex and money flow from the same wellspring of imaginary desire." *The two monastic vows—that of abstinence and that of poverty—are precisely related by being against*

that common wellspring of imaginary desire and,

therefore, one cannot keep one of the vows without also keeping the other.]

Fragment 27

There is a point of ambiguity here, one that needs to be raised in relation to the Prologue of the *Republic* and specifically to that little scene where Adeimantus and Polemarchus "persuade" Socrates to stay in the Piraeus by appealing to his tripartite desire (*voir, avoir, savoir*). The question is: What role does sex play in the *polis*? Book I of the *Republic* seems to suggest that at least the head of the city is to be like Cephalus—but that's rather impossible, if he is also to be a *philo*-sopher or *philo*-anything for that matter; a point that sustains an ongoing contradiction within the Platonic vision of the king who is a lover of wisdom but otherwise unerotic.

Yet, what Adeimantus and Polemarchus prove by "arresting" Socrates—the otherwise unaffected philosopher and therefore the exemplary idea of the ruling philosopher— arresting him, *not* by force, but by *desire*, is that desire, and specifically *eros* as the principle desire, is a political force of its own and that,

even though it can be volatile and dangerous
to the regime (think of Harmodius and Aris-
togeiton), so too can it be useful when used
knowingly (here, the reader might desire to
return to the *Charmides*). Desire can be used
precisely as it is used in Aristophanes' speech
in the *Symposium*: sex is the ἄλλην μηχανήν intro-
duced by gods (191b5-6) as a remedy (φάρμακον)
or as solution (λύσις) to the human ἀργία (191b)
that came as a result of their dichotomy. Sex in
these pages of the *Symposium* is an expedient
capable of bringing the half-creatures back
from the melancholy of desire to the business
of life, specifically, to that of work (ἐπὶ τὰ ἔργα).

Fragment 28

From the understanding of sex as the remedy to ἀργία and as the force behind the production (and reproduction) of work, the slogan "make love, not war" cannot make sense except as a capitalist imperative. War, after all, is disruptive to the business as usual that allows the agora to take control of the city. War, not sex, is orgiastic and orgasmic.

Fragment 29

A very common and to some extent understandable mistake in general, but one which has significant ramifications when it comes to sex in particular, is the confusion between imagination and reality whereby the imaginary is taken for the real. (Clemente ought to pay particular attention to this point). I speak of sexual fantasies that one sadly mistakes as existing only in the safety of one's imagination, fantasies one would not dare to actualize in reality, either because one finds them detestable (disregarding, as so often happens, the apparent contradiction implied by detesting what one finds attractive) or because such desires are forbidden in the "real world" on the authority of law or religion.

Such a distinction, however, cannot be trusted. For, it fails to comprehend what imagination is. It mistakenly thinks that imagination does nothing more than copy her fertile twin sister, reality, as she herself is unable to bring forth offspring of her own, such as sexual fantasies, which—and this is a truth each of us must find out for himself—would immediately scatter and vanish under the atmospheric pressure of the real. That is to say that the pleasure one derives from sexual fantasy consists precisely in its being *imagined*. It is pleasurable only insofar as it is imagined. Even the pleasure one derives from reality is not, if close attention is paid, experienced (felt/lived) *in* reality but *in* imagination. It is the pleasure of an anticipation given to us by imagination and, as soon as it has happened, the pleasure of an imaginary recollection.

Fragment 30

The retreat to privacy.
Privacy is a condition for the sexual act, otherwise exhibitionism would not be a paraphilia. It is as if we feel the need to hide most when we are about to hide ourselves from ourselves. Sex involves a double cover-up: I hide from others as I am about to escape, always only briefly, myself. And should anyone, therefore, enter my hiding place and catch me *in flagrante delicto*? What would be there for him to see? Something, perhaps, but no-one. Something, but not someone.

[Nota bene: *Something similar happens when one sins. Sin, after all, is an invisibility, a momentary lapse away from God's sustaining "memory," a self-effacement, for which, nevertheless, one feels the need to hide as one is hiding from His face.*]

Fragment 31

Whom do you embrace when you are embracing your sexual partner? Who is this other whose body mirrors yours so symmetrically, limb by limb? Doesn't this very mirroring make you suspicious that, to you and for you, this other body in your arms is only an embodied phantasy of yours? A figment of your imagination or of your past ("sex is the nostalgia for sex" says the prophet of pop art) that has been summoned by means that resemble magic and has been dressed in soft flesh and warm blood for a little while before returning to himself once more?

This power of sex to eclipse the other under the guise of desire is in fact so great that we can venture to say that *sex is the safest place to hide from the other.*

Fragment 32

We are never ourselves during sex, never our public selves, our egos. This means that in another sense we are ourselves only during sex. The question that no one, to my knowledge, has asked, even though we have asked plenty of other questions when it comes to this subject, and we are always ready to ask more, the question that needs to be asked (and, if possible, be answered as well) before every other is: *who* is it who has sex when one is having sex?

If, as Borges suggests, "all men who repeat a line from Shakespeare *are* William Shakespeare," then it must follow that all men, in the vertiginous moment of coitus, are the same man. Namely, no-one.

Fragment 33

Sexual desire—or perhaps pre-sexual desire that is later codified as sexual and, precisely by this codification, becomes what we call *sexual desire*—is a process of fossilizing childhood (or, more precisely, of fossilizing our first discovery of sexual desire during childhood). By examining how one derives pleasure later in life, as an "adult," one learns a great deal about the child one once was.

Fragment 34

Is pleasure, then, the pleasure of returning to one's childhood—a nostalgia for the child I once was? The pleasure of sex indeed lies in what amounts to a momentary return to childhood, in becoming brutal like a child and innocent like an animal, closer to the animal kingdom than to civilized humanity and thus free (or so one imagines) not only from the burden of one's own existence but also from society's restrictions.

The following passage from Musil's *The Man Without Qualities* comes to mind: "He had never yet perceived as clearly as in the instant he followed her into bed how much the passionate intrusion into another body is a sequel to a child's liking for secret and forbidden hiding places."

Fragment 35

Sex oscillates between the childish and the child-like.

The expression in Greek literature for what a man typically desires is τὰ παιδικά (Zeno of Elea was, for example, τὰ παιδικά of Parmenides (see, *Parmenides*, 127b5)). Today the same expression can be used in a more literal sense as referring to sex as childish: τὰ παιδικά— what is characteristic of or proper to children. In other words, "When I was a child, I talked like a child, I thought like a child" (1 Cor. 13:11). But when one grows up, he is expected to "put the ways of the child behind [him]."

Fragment 36

Sexual excitation does not consist of, is not provoked or in any way caused by sex. Rather violence, re-enacted and re-presented in the sexual act in all its variations, is the real witches' brew. One could call it a rousing mixture of "sensuality and cruelty," as Nietzsche does, but it is violence all the same. And I don't mean just the select cases where the violence is obvious (slapping, biting, spanking, hair pulling, or even the non-physical abuse of verbal humiliation). I mean even something as "innocent" as kissing, which, if regarded properly, barely disguises the desire to devour the other.

The difficulty—and the moral obligation, if you fashion yourself a moralist, my friend—is to refuse to dismiss this observation, either by the futile and hypocritical distinction between "good" sex (conjugal or at least nuptial, loving, perhaps even romantic) and "bad" sex (perverted, abusive, animalistic), or by the even more ambitious and even more futile attempt to introduce such a distinction within violence itself ("sacred" violence, sacrifice, vs. destruction). The task here is to understand why for human beings, violence implies "intimacy." Is it perhaps that love includes the desire to make the other one's own and the means by which we do so is taking possession of the other, owning him like an object? If so, perhaps "sexual violence" is man's attempt to lay claim over the other—and of course, nothing proves that one owns something more than one's liberty to use it and misuse it as one wishes.

Here we discover a connection between love and liberty—that is, the liberty of *rights*, the right to use, the right to property. When Masetto, in Mozart's *Don Giovanni*, suspects that his newly-wed wife, Zerlina, has been cheating on him (and on the day of their wedding, no less!), all Zerlina can do to prove that she has been faithful is ask him, beg him, to beat her:

Beat me, beat me, my Masetto!
Beat your poor Zerlina!
I'll stay here like a little lamb,
And await your every blow.
Beat, beat your poor Zerlina!
I'll let you pull my hair out,
I'll let you gouge my eyes out,
And then happily I will kiss,
Your wonderfully sweet hands!
(Act I, scene 4)

How fitting it seems that cruelty is the language
of tenderness, the language of love. We see this
in Proust. We see it every day out our windows.
A sweet cruelty. Nothing says "you are mine"
more than the license we give ourselves to tor-
ture our beloved with words—and, in the bedroom, with physical pain as well. (*Batti, batti, o
bell Masetto*).

Fragment 37

One must be willfully blind if one refuses to see that sex is about violence. (I've put it this way so as to avoid saying what would have been more accurate, but also more provocative, namely, that *sex is intrinsically violent*). In oral sex, for instance, what one is dealing with is a desire to eat one's partner raw. (*Omophagia* was, incidentally, one of only two fundamental characteristics of the religious worship of Dionysus; the other was *sparagmos*). And the opposite of raw, in the binary opposition which has been described by Claude Lévi-Strauss, is *cooked*—a term that belongs, shall we say, in the kitchen? So, what does it mean to find in one's bedroom the language of the kitchen?

Fragment 38

There is little doubt that people decide to get married "initially and for the most part" for the convenience of having the possibility of sex readily available at any hour, day or night, in the comfort of their own homes. But later, I suspect, a greater pleasure arises on account of which the desire for sex fades, and that is the pleasure of being able to be mean to another person with relative impunity, the freedom from the societal constraints of politeness one experiences in marital life. (Politeness, to follow Heidegger, is really just a mask for indifference and as such, it thrives on distance, disinterest, and disregard—better, then, to disregard it). At home, where one is supposed to be *at home*, at home with oneself, one must be oneself. This is the difference between the *spouse* and the *other*—around a spouse one can be oneself without having to fear one will offend public decorum by doing so. This is what is meant by "familiarity"—a term that originates from and refers back to the family.

Strangely, and all due attention must be given to this point, sex does not confer the freedom of familiarity. It is only by means of cohabitation over an extended period of time that one comes to earn the freedom to be one's miserable self, earn it by allowing one's partner to be miserably himself as well. Man, however, is a selfish animal and to live with another is a daily schooling in self-resignation. Matrimony, which to my French ear sounds confusingly like martyrdom, should perhaps be recoined *martyrmony*.

Fragment 39

Whether sex is or is not sinful is not for me to decide. But I do think that one thing about sex—our preoccupation with it—deserves to be called sinful and avoided at all costs. This includes thinking and writing about sex. It is a good thing, therefore, that this book has come to an end and to this end in particular—that is, an end that concludes by bringing to our attention the fact that sex is not worth thinking about and that to do so is as infantile as sex itself.

What is more, I suspect that the moralist's insistence that we drag sin into the conversation is nothing more than a cunning ruse. For, by doing so we invest sex with the same ambiguity which is characteristic of sin and even begin to gesture at God's mysterious ways, so that, by debating what God thinks of sex—whether he views it as sinful or not—we can hold off endlessly that moment when we need to make up our minds and assume our responsibility for what we think (and write) about it.

Fragment 40

At the end, one might still expect a clear and unambiguous answer to the problem of sex, if not a judgment on sex and on human sexuality more broadly. Such a response, if it were possible, would be rendered useless, however, the moment it was pronounced because it would be so universal and abstract that it would not be applicable to the particular circumstances in which we find human sexuality. There are experiences that refuse to conform to our definitions, you know. There are actions that defy our concepts.

Consider: just as there is a qualitative difference between giving to a beggar while thinking that you are his savior and giving to a beggar while thinking that *he* is *your* savior (or that he might as well be your Savior)—even if, seen from without, both of these acts appear to be the same—so too is there a fundamental difference between sex pursued as an arena for boasting of one's skills of seduction and sex understood as the field of truth (Plato's πεδίον τῆς ἀληθείας) in which one finds oneself defeated by one's vulnerability. Nothing in the "externals" of the two attitudes suggests their difference, yet they are worlds apart. If the former is perhaps to be called sinful, because selfish, then one must make an exemption for the latter, which might even become, in God's hands, a tributary of holiness.

Hors-Série
Theotokion

Resistance to the Virgin Mary, even enmity and blasphemy against her, might be explained by the fact that she as a woman—but also as the Virgin who is, paradoxically a Mother—makes inescapable the reference to the human body and, in particular, to a female body—that is, the kind of body that is traditionally and universally eroticized, even if only to bless "the womb that bore [Him] and the breast at which [He] nursed" (Luke 11:27). As it happens, the reproductive organs are also the sexual organs and, therefore, the Virgin Mary insists on reminding us of what we would prefer to repress and forget. She reminds us of what we pretend to have forgotten. She is the embodiment of that reminder and it might therefore make some sense that some people, in their urgency to keep their little shameful secret, would go so far as to eclipse her by resolving, one way or another, the tension between

Virginity and Motherhood, sanctity and sexuality, and thus hide her, and themselves, from their eyes.

Postscript
A Retraction

How wrong I was in "Dying to Desire"! Right—for my description was accurate, but wrong in the conclusions I drew on the basis of that description. Sex *is* violent through and through but that doesn't mean that its violence makes it as dark and gloomy as I made it out to be in that essay. Or rather it *could* mean that for as long as one is standing *outside*. Looked upon from without, sex must be either ridiculous or perverse. But from the inside, so to speak, sexual violence (and by that I mean the violence that is acted out between sexual partners in their desire to—in their words—pound, tear, and eat, and in short, perform all kinds of violence upon the Other) speaks of something entirely different and, perhaps, even higher; it speaks of sex's affinity with orgiastic religion.

Together with sex, violence is endemic to religion, most notably, of course, in sacrifice. In this sense, one would be right to speak of "religious violence" which is different from what one usually understands by the expression. For, in sacrifice too one pounds, tears, and eats the Other. So, what I saw when writing that essay was accurate, but I paid no attention to (I did not notice) where I was standing. I was standing, like Pentheus in the *Bacchae* (that is, as a voyeur) *outside* the experience I sought to describe. And, as Professor Beauchard has so rightly said, from the outside sex cannot but appear offensive, that is, it cannot fail to offend us. It is *offensive* in the way Kierkegaard understood the term. And so, the synchronous coincidence of myself with my younger self *in persona* of the Beloved does not mean, as I argued then, that all sexual desire is, in essence, necrophilia; rather, it ought to have been taken as something analogous to those epiphanic moments of involuntary memories that Proust describes as the singular experience that motivated and enabled his work, but also, as the experience which infused him with "pure joy."

John Panteleimon Manoussakis
The College of the Holy Cross
2nd Friday after Pascha
April 28, 2023